KU-480-883

The Cat Lover's Coffee Table Book

Written and compiled by

NANETTE NEWMAN
and GRAHAM TARRANT

Drawings by EDWARD MCLACHLAN

COLLINS 8 Grafton Street, London 1983

For Queenie and Rex

ACKNOWLEDGEMENTS
Room with a Cat (page 8)
From *Moncrif's Cats* (translated by Reginald Bretnor), published by
The Golden Cockerel Press, 1961

Writer's Moll (page 11)
Letter from *Raymond Chandler Speaking*, edited by Dorothy Gardiner
and Kathrine Sorley Walker, published by Hamish Hamilton, 1962

Faith Healing (page 20)
From *The Diary of a Country Parson* by James Woodforde, edited by
John Beresford (abridged edition, 1978), © Oxford University
Press 1978. By permission of Oxford University Press.

William Collins Sons & Co Ltd
London · Glasgow · Sydney · Auckland
Toronto · Johannesburg

British Library Cataloguing in Publication Data

Newman, Nanette
 The cat lover's coffee-table book.
 1. Cats—Anecdotes, facetiae, satire, etc.
 I. Title II. Tarrant, Graham
 636.8′0207   SF442

ISBN 0–00–216453–1

First published 1983
© in the text Bryan Forbes Limited and Graham Tarrant 1983
© in the illustrations Edward McLachlan 1983

Photoset in Baskerville
Made and Printed in Great Britain by
Robert Hartnoll Ltd, Bodmin

CAT: A soft indestructible automaton provided by nature to be kicked when things go wrong in the domestic circle.

Ambrose Bierce, *The Devil's Dictionary*

CAT: A domestick animal that catches mice, commonly reckoned by naturalists the lowest order of the leonine species.

Dr Samuel Johnson, *Dictionary of the English Language*

CAT: One hell of a nice animal, frequently mistaken for a meatloaf.

B. Kliban, *Cat*

AHARRR, JIM LADS...

Pussy Footing

When a cat belonging to the eminent surgeon Sir Arbuthnot Lane
was run over in the street, the good doctor himself operated on the
animal and amputated its crushed front paw. The cat survived the
ordeal and thereafter happily hopped about on three legs. Later
it gave birth to kittens, who, thinking it was the done thing, raised
the corresponding front paw off the ground and dutifully followed
in their mother's footsteps.

The kitten is in the animal world what the rosebud is in the garden.
(ROBERT SOUTHEY)

Awayday

When the fast train from Crewe pulled into Shrewsbury station one day in 1962, the driver found two kittens huddled together on the engine, just inches from the front wheels. They had miraculously survived the thirty-two-mile journey at sixty miles per hour, arriving at their destination shaken but not stirred.

Scaredy Cats

A cat may look at a king, but two kings at least couldn't bear looking at cats. The sixteenth-century dog-loving Henry III of France, who would take his puppies for a walk around Paris in a basket hanging from his neck, was terrified of cats. While the great Napoleon, conqueror of half Europe, would tremble and break out in a cold sweat at the sight of even a tiny kitten.

Kings and others who have an unreasonable fear of cats are known as ailurphobes. Cats who can't stand kings are called republicans.

ARRÊTEZ..... MON JOLI..... MON PETIT WELLINGTON....

In Japan the cat is called 'the tiger that eats from the hand'.

ROOM WITH A CAT

Sometimes a fondness for Cats is carried to the extreme. This past Autumn in a little village called Passy, situated on the Evreux route, a Lady who came from Paris with a great retinue, arrived very late at a very mediocre Hostelry; her first care before descending from her carriage was to demand if there was a Cat in the house; they told her there was not; but they promised her marvels in all other respects; she replied that there had to be a Cat for her, and that without one she would not be able to stay; they at once went to wake the whole village, and they finally brought her the female Cat of the Curé's; as soon as she had taken her up in her arms, the Lady entered the Hostelry and believed herself in the Palace of Psyche. She vowed that whenever she passed the night in an apartment where there was no Cat at all, she was seized by insupportable vapours. Her health suffered badly whenever she was away; she was reduced to borrowing one at each stop she made and whenever she could find none, she passed the night in the open.

From MONCRIF's CATS, translated by Reginald Bretnor

(THIRTEENTH-CENTURY PROVERB)

UNHAPPY LANDINGS

Drop a cat in an upside-down position from a height of one foot and within a split second it will right itself and land harmlessly on its paws. Unfortunately the same can't be said of the 85,000 cats a year that fall, jump or are pushed out of American skyscrapers. New York vets call this disturbing phenomenon the 'high rise syndrome', but for most of the cats it is nothing less than journey's end.

Writer's Moll

The books of Raymond Chandler are full of people being mugged, maimed or murdered; but the quality the writer admired most in his cat Taki, a beautiful black Persian, was the compassion she showed towards her victims. As he wrote to a friend:

> She has another curious trick (which may or may not be rare) of never killing anything. She brings 'em back alive and lets you take them away from her. She has brought into the house at various times such things as a dove, a blue parrakeet, and a large butterfly. The butterfly and the parrakeet were entirely unharmed and carried on just as though nothing had happened. The dove gave her a little trouble and had a small spot of blood on its breast, but we took it to a bird man and it was all right very soon. Just a bit humiliated. Mice bore her, but she catches them if they insist and then I have to kill them.

Taki was Chandler's constant companion. He referred to her as his 'secretary', because of her habit of sitting on his manuscripts or leaning against the typewriter as he sent private eye Philip Marlowe and others about their violent business. She lived for almost twenty years. Then, sadly, for Taki it was a case of the big sleep and . . . farewell, my lovely!

A friend of Dorothy Parker's once asked her advice on how to have an ailing cat put down. 'Try curiosity' was the reply.

NATIONAL SERVICE

To protect his army's food supplies from marauding rats and mice, Frederick the Great recruited cats as sentries. Whenever he occupied a town or village during one of his campaigns, he would force the local citizens to drum up a new brigade of feline guards. There are no contemporary reports to show how well the cats adjusted to the rigours of army life, but at least one military exercise must have come as second nature to them. Digging the latrines.

Who will not feed the cats, must feed the mice and rats.

(GERMAN PROVERB)

Diamonds are Forever

Ming-Ling, a Burmese cat, swallowed a diamond and ruby ring
worth £3,200. An X-ray revealed that it had lodged
in the cat's abdominal cavity, but Ming-Ling's owner
refused to allow a vet to operate, saying that if the ring
didn't pass through the animal's system naturally,
it could be removed at leisure after the cat's death.
For a while Ming-Ling was guarded day and night
by a private detective employed by the insurance company.
The minder slept on a couch in the drawing-room with
the cat by his side; if for some reason he had to leave
the house, Ming-Ling was incarcerated in the cellar.

Eventually the insurance company gave it up as a bad job,
withdrawing both the detective and their cover.
From then on, Ming-Ling was condemned to a lifetime
on a lead until the gem was safely deposited.

Embassy Defector

Before the US Ambassador to the Soviet Union, Llewellyn E. Thompson, returned home on leave in 1962, he left strict instructions with his staff concerning his cat, Kitty. Each night someone was to sleep with her in the ambassadorial bed as she hated sleeping alone, and on no account was she to be allowed outside the Residence. But no sooner was Mr Llewellyn's back turned than Kitty made good her escape, cleverly using the occasion of a diplomatic party to slip past the preoccupied guards on the front gate.

As soon as her departure was discovered, the Embassy staff leapt into action. The Russian police were called in and the biggest cat-hunt that Moscow has ever known got underway. Recognizing that this was a true emergency, the British, America's closest ally, despatched a number of personnel to join in the search. In the hours that followed dozens of cats answering Kitty's description were snatched off the streets and brought to the Embassy for identification, but to no avail.

Then at 2 a.m., just when it seemed as if Kitty was one cat who wouldn't be coming in from the cold, a policeman ran triumphantly up the drive. His right wrist was scratched and bleeding, but tucked firmly under his arm in a powerful headlock was the defiant and struggling form of the Ambassador's cat. One of the most senior animals in the American diplomatic service had been found seeking asylum in a shop doorway.

FLASH IN THE PAN

The Kitty Whiz Kit invented by an Illinois company teaches a cat how to use its owner's toilet. The cat sits (*sic*) on a plastic attachment which is fitted over the standard loo seat. Toilet training takes just a few days through a process the manufacturers enigmatically describe as 'successive approximation'.

Upstaged

When Dame Edith Evans played Miss Betsy in a filmed
version of *David Copperfield*, there was a scene
where she had a long speech to deliver while carrying
a cat in a basket. The director thought it expedient to ask
the studio vet to sedate the cat before shooting
the scene, but as often happens on a
film set there was a considerable delay before
everything was ready, and the effects of the tranquillizer
wore off. Dame Edith was in full flight when
the cat came to and started to struggle to get out of
the basket. Being too disciplined a professional
to let a mere animal steal her thunder,
Dame Edith pushed the cat firmly back with
her hand and, without a discernible pause in her
flow of words, interpolated, 'Don't be
such an ambitious pussy!
You're not in *Dick Whittington*!'
And then reverted to
the script without so much
as a flicker.

Confound the cats! All cats – alway –
Cats of all colours, black, white, grey;
By night a nuisance and by day –
Confound the cats!

ORLANDO DOBBIN, *A Dithyramb on Cats*

Faith Healing

From the diary of Parson Woodforde, 26 October 1768:

I had a poor little cat, that had one of her ribs broke and that laid across her belly, and we could not tell what it was, and she was in great pain. I therefore with a small pen knife this morning, opened one side of her and took it out, and performed the operation very well, and afterwards sewed it up and put Friars Balsam to it, and she was much better after. . . .

The Diary of a Country Parson 1758–1802 by James Woodforde

HOLY CATS

The Middle Ages apart, when for a while the fur undoubtedly hit the fan, some of the Church's best friends have been cats. The prophet Mohammed, for example, when preparing to go to his devotions, once cut off the sleeve of his robe on which his cat, Muezza, was dozing rather than disturb the animal. The nineteenth-century Pope Leo XII was another great cat lover. His favourite, a tabby christened Micetto, was born in the Vatican and reared in the Pontiff's garments, and like his master abstemiously avoided eating meat. On his deathbed Pope Leo bequeathed Micetto to his friend, the French writer Chateaubriand.

In England Cardinal Wolsey, who presided over the divorce of Henry VIII and Katharine of Aragon, refused to be separated from his own cat, taking it to banquets, state functions and even, on occasions, into the pulpit with him.

But the fourteen cats of Cardinal Richlieu were less fortunate. During the lifetime of the most powerful man in France, the animals were waited on by servants and fed a diet of chicken pâté and other delicacies; and generous provision was made in the Cardinal's will for their life of luxury to continue after his death. But when Richlieu eventually died in 1642 the allegiance of his personal army of Swiss Guards died with him. Far from obeying his instructions concerning the cats, the guards rounded up all fourteen of the poor creatures and destroyed them.

A man who loves cats will marry an immoral woman. (FRENCH PROVERB)

Moslem Riddle

Question: Why do cats close their eyes when drinking milk?

Answer: So that when Allah asks them if they have had some, they can say (paw on heart) that they haven't seen any milk. And so qualify for another dishful.

Speaking the Language

Give or take an accent or two, the French, Germans,
Italians, Russians, Swedes, Norwegians, Israelis and apostles
of Esperanto are all agreed that the sound a cat makes
is miaow. *The odd tongue out is Japanese which*
can't make up its mind if the animal says
nyah-nyah *or* mi-mi. *Perhaps one of them*
is computer language.

It is a very inconvenient habit of kittens
(Alice had once made the remark)
that, whatever you say to them, they
always purr.

(Lewis Carroll,
Through the Looking Glass)

PAY PAWS

Rufus, the official mouser at the Treasury in the 1920s, was paid at the rate of tuppence a day, with all the mice he could catch as a bonus. Not a great reward for someone who had the responsibility of keeping acres of rooms and miles of corridor rodent-free. So when a recommendation for a fifty per cent pay rise for him was turned down by the Treasury chiefs, Rufus's labour was withdrawn.

The matter was referred to the Chancellor of the Exchequer, Philip Snowden, a man not noted for his generosity on Budget Days but with a good track record when it came to animals. He summoned the cat to a meeting in his office and after much leg rubbing, head nuzzling and purring (it's not known what Rufus did) agreed to the increase. The negotiations successfully concluded, Mr Snowden returned to the problems of unemployment and inflation – and Rufus went back to taxing the mice.

Wild Cat Strike

In 1975 twenty-one British Leyland workers walked off the job because of the overpowering smell of stray cats at the factory. As a result a further 600 men had to be laid off.

Wet and Windy

It's an old superstition that if a cat washing itself raises its leg above its head, there will soon be rain. And in Scotland, when a cat scratches a table-leg the chances are it will rustle up a gale.

Boswell's Life of Hodge

Nothing in Samuel Johnson's life escaped the attention of his friend James Boswell, including his love of cats:

I never shall forget the indulgence with which he treated Hodge, his cat; for whom he himself used to go out and buy oysters, lest the servants having that trouble should take a dislike to the poor creature. I am, unluckily, one of those who have an antipathy to a cat, so that I am uneasy when in the room with one; and I own, I frequently suffered a good deal from the presence of this same Hodge. I recollect him one day scrambling up Dr Johnson's breast, apparently with much satisfaction, while my friend smiling and half-whistling, rubbed down his back, and pulled him by the tail; and when I observed he was a fine cat, saying 'why yes, Sir, but I have had cats whom I liked better than this;' and then as if perceiving Hodge to be out of countenance, adding, 'but he is a very fine cat, a very fine cat indeed.'

From *The Life of Samuel Johnson* (1783) by JAMES BOSWELL

There was an amusing footnote to this story when in 1964 the City of London Festival re-enacted Hodge and his oyster eating on stage. Sixty felines were auditioned for the part, which eventually went to an eleven-year-old acting cat called Mitten, at wages of one pound an hour. The female Mitten had little difficulty playing the male Hodge, except for one thing: she hated oysters. However like any good pro Mitten knew that the show must go on, even if it meant bringing the oysters up after the curtain came down.

DICK'S CAT

The cat that made Dick Whittington's fortune was not an animal but a boat. London's most famous Lord Mayor and principal boy struck it rich by shipping coal from Newcastle to London in special cargo vessels called *cats* (the name is derived from a Scandinavian word and has nothing whatsoever to do with moggies). Just how the feline variety got into the legendary act isn't clear, though who would pay to see a pantomime about a coal merchant?

A cat who walked upright in boots
Took to gambling and smoking cheroot
He played a guitar
And drove a fast car
And Yves St Laurent made his suits.

If the cat had wings she'd
choke all the birds in
the air.
(YIDDISH PROVERB)

Bird-watcher

A lady had a tame bird which she was in the habit of letting out
of its cage every day. One morning as it was picking crumbs of
bread off the carpet, her cat, who always before showed great
kindness for the bird, seized it on a sudden, and jumped with it
in her mouth upon a table. The lady was much alarmed for the
fate of her favourite, but on turning about instantly discerned
the cause. The door had been left open, and a strange cat had
just come into the room! After turning it out, her own cat came
down from her place of safety, and dropped the bird without
having done it the smallest injury.

Nineteenth-century anecdote.

Vote Catchers

In 1949 the Illinois State Legislature passed a bill which would punish cat owners for permitting their animals to roam free, and allowed for the use of cat traps by the authorities. Cats were described as a public nuisance and a menace, in particular, to song birds.

To the relief of the beleaguered cat owners (and their cats), however, Governor Adlai Stevenson vetoed the bill, saying: 'I cannot agree that it should be the declared public policy of Illinois that a cat visiting a neighbour's yard or crossing the highway is a public nuisance. It is in the nature of cats to do a certain amount of unescorted roaming. . . . The problem of the cat versus the bird is as old as time. If we attempt to resolve it by legislation, who knows but what we may be called upon to take sides as well in the age-old problems of dog versus cat, bird versus bird, or even bird versus worm. In my opinion, the State of Illinois and its governing bodies already have enough to do without trying to control feline delinquency.'

Cat-loving Adlai Stevenson was twice defeated in the race for the American Presidency by cat-hating Dwight D. Eisenhower, who once ordered that any cat seen in the grounds of his home in Gettysburg should be shot. Something he omitted to mention in any of his election speeches.

Of all God's creatures there is only one that cannot be made the slave of the lash. That one is the cat. If man could be crossed with the cat it would improve man, but it would deteriorate the cat.　(MARK TWAIN)

Maxi Cats

In the sixties, a London organization called Spook Enterprises launched a 'Maxi Cat Project'. The plan was to reproduce domestic cats at twice their normal size to sell to witches as familiars. Spook wouldn't say what their magic formula was, but at a guess it involved double, double toil and trouble – and no small amount of hot air.

Gone Fishin'

When Horace Walpole's cat Selima was drowned in a 'tub of gold fishes', his friend, the poet Thomas Gray, penned in her memory the celebrated 'Ode on the Death of a Favourite Cat'. The poem contains the immortal lines:

> What female heart can gold despise?
> What cat's averse to fish?

and ends with the warning:

> Not all that tempts
>   your wand'ring eyes
> And heedless hearts,
>   is lawful prize;
> Nor all that glisters, gold.

Name Dropping

As T. S. Eliot poetically observed, 'the Naming of Cats is a difficult matter'. But when it comes to the matter writers, especially poets, take a lot of beating. Sir Walter Scott bestowed on his favourite feline the catchy title of Hinse of Hinsefield. French novelist and poet Théophile Gautier went in for alliteration with Zizi, Zulema, Zuleika and Zobeide. While there was more than a touch of the nursery rhymes about the nomenclature of English poet Thomas Hood's cat, Tabitha Longclaws Tiddlywink, and her three kittens, Pepperpot, Scratchaway and Sootikins.

But for literary quantity the prize must go to the nineteenth-century Poet Laureate Robert Southey, who christened his cat 'The Most Noble the Archduke Rumpelstilzchen, Marquis Macbum, Earle Tomemange, Baron Raticide, Waowler, and Skaratchi'. To save time, the animal also answered to the name of 'Rumpel'.

They say that the test of literary power is whether a man can write an inscription.
I say, 'Can he name a kitten?'

(SAMUEL BUTLER)

Confucius Says

The cat who has an extra mousehole in the range of its eye is less likely to go hungry than the cat with its whiskers stuck patiently in one mousehole only.

Share and Share Alike

Agnes Repplier, in her cat classic *The Fireside Sphinx*, published in 1901, tells the story of 'an English cat who was fed daily at the family dinner hour, receiving from his master's hand choice bits of fish and fowl. On a certain winter evening he was unaccountably absent from his post; but when the dinner was half served, he came rushing up the stairs, carrying two mice in his mouth. One he dropped upon his own platter, and then, before he could be stopped, he leaped upon the table, and deposited the second on his master's plate – a graceful and pretty, however unwelcome, attention, and one which plainly showed a well-bred desire to requite the hospitality he had received.'

The cat in gloves catches no mice. (ENGLISH PROVERB)

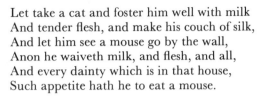

Let take a cat and foster him well with milk
And tender flesh, and make his couch of silk,
And let him see a mouse go by the wall,
Anon he waiveth milk, and flesh, and all,
And every dainty which is in that house,
Such appetite hath he to eat a mouse.

GEOFFREY CHAUCER, *The Maunciple's Tale*

PERFORMING CATS

Professor Frederick and his troupe of twelve performing cats – all Angoras bred in Spain – made a much-publicized tour of Britain in 1885. As part of their act the animals would run across the top of a line of Champagne bottles, climb up and down a flagpole, and leap through a blazing hoop. But it was the bizarre *pièce de résistance* that created the greatest sensation. To the accompaniment of a drum roll one of the cats would gingerly make its way across a tightrope, at intervals along which a number of live mice, rats and canaries were stationed. The audience held its breath as the cat clambered over each of the obstacles in turn without 'ruffling their serenity or alarming their sensibilities'.

The professor was more than happy to disclose to the Press the training secrets of his stunt cats, but there was no explanation forthcoming on the ice-cool performance of the other creatures. Perhaps it was simply fear that kept them frozen to the spot.

Wedding Bells

In New York in 1963 a wedding took place between a Chinchilla Persian called Babyface and Nicodemus, a handsome Silver Persian. The bride wore a white net gown and the groom sported top hat and tails, one of which was his own. The service was conducted by a beagle and the matron-of-honour was another Persian cat. A special kitty cake was baked for the wedding breakfast and the happy couple were toasted in cream.

It is said that if a cat sneezes in front of a bride on her wedding day, the marriage will be a happy one. But in France, a girl who treads on a cat's tail will take a year longer to find a husband.

Dear Puss...

WELCOME TO CATIFORNIA

In California they do their best to cater for the cat community. For those mollycoddled moggies whose owners can afford it, there is a cat department store, a cat holiday resort, a cat rest home, a cat massage parlour, a cat maternity home, a cat dating service, a rent-a-cat agency, cat acting coaches, cat psychics and cat psychiatrists. One Los Angeles store has even splashed out with water beds for cats, which only a wet blanket would disapprove of.

But in at least one aspect of cat care the Sunshine State has been eclipsed. A pet motel in Illinois – the last miaow in comfort – makes a point of reading aloud to its feline guests letters sent them by their absent owners. Hopefully the cats are not too moved by the experience to scratch out a reply.

Cats seem to go on the principle that it never does any harm to ask for what you want.

(JOSEPH WOOD KRUTCH)

HORROR STORY

Once upon a time (in 1975 to be exact) an old hotel in Sudbury, Suffolk, was being redeveloped. The builders working on the site dug up the 300-year-old remains of a mummified cat which had been buried there, as was the custom 300 years ago, to ward off evil spirits. This was the innocent prelude to a series of strange and frightening events.

First the development company ran out of money and had to withdraw from the project. Then the premises where the cat's body was being housed mysteriously burned down, though the cat came through the experience unsinged. After that the gruesome package was removed to a nearby farmhouse, but that too went up in flames, with the cat once again turning out to be fireproof. Back went the cat to the hotel – but not before the builder carrying it in his car was involved in a serious road accident – and in fell the brand new roof. Worse, the hitherto solid oak beams suddenly and unaccountably shifted, putting a further £60,000 on the bill.

The desperate owners, at last seeing the light, sent for the local vicar, who performed a burial service on what was left of the seventeenth-century moggy. As a peace offering, a note was placed inside the coffin apologizing for the disturbance. There were no more problems from that moment on. The rest of the construction work was completed on time, and business at the hotel prospered happily ever after.

That is, until someone else puts the cat out.

Singed cats live long.
(YIDDISH PROVERB)

Hoddley, poddley puddle and fogs
The cats are to marry the poodle dogs
Cats in blue jackets and dogs in red hats
What will become of the mice and the rats?

(Traditional nursery rhyme)

CAT RULES OK?

In a letter to a friend, Sir Walter Scott described how his new and later most famous dog, Maida, was getting on with the cat of the house, Hinse of Hinsefield.

I have added a most romantic inmate to my family – a large bloodhound, allowed to be the finest dog of the kind in Scotland, perfectly gentle, affectionate and good-natured, and the darling of all the children. He is between the deer-greyhound and mastiff, with a shaggy mane like a lion, and always sits beside me at dinner, his head as high as the back of my chair. Yet it will gratify you to know that a favourite cat keeps him in the greatest possible order, insists upon all rights of precedence, and scratches with impunity the nose of an animal who would make no bones of a wolf, and pulls down a red deer without fear or difficulty. I heard my friend set up some most piteous howls, and I assure you the noise was no joke, all occasioned by his fear of passing Puss, who had stationed himself on the stairs. . . .

Heads and Tails

At the last count there were an astonishing thirty-four million
cats residing in the USA. That's roughly one for every
six humans. In the UK the figure is just over five
millions, a ratio of one to eleven. But for 250,000
stray cats – the largest vagrant population in the
world – there's no place like Rome.

No matter how much cats fight, there always seem
to be plenty of kittens.

(ABRAHAM LINCOLN)

MUMMY CATS

Cats were worshipped in Ancient Egypt. To kill one, even acciden-tally, meant certain death – and not only for the cat. The powerful sun god Ra was often depicted in feline form, and the sensual goddess Bastet (Bast for short) was shown as having a woman's body with a cat's head. Sacred cats, supposed to be incarnations of Bastet, were kept in her temple at Bubastis. The animals were watched over by priests who interpreted their signs – a purr here, a scratch there – to make and sell predictions, a profitable sideline for any goddess. When the cats died, they were mummified and ceremoniously buried alongside the temple, often with embalmed mice thrown in for afterworld meals.

In the nineteenth century, when another of Bastet's temples was excavated, 300,000 mummified cats were dug up. They were shipped to Liverpool and Manchester and sold as fertilizer at four pounds a ton. A fate the cats never predicted.

Cat Nap

An elderly English cat, who was dozing one day before the nursery fire, was disturbed and annoyed by the whining of a fretful child. The cat, who had reared several large families of her own, bore the noise as long as it could, waiting for the nurse to interpose her authority. Then, finding passive endurance had outstripped the limits of her patience, she arose, crossed the room, jumped on the sofa, and twice with her strong soft paw, which had chastised many an erring kitten, deliberately boxed the little girl's ears – after which they both re-turned to their slumbers.

NINETEENTH-CENTURY ANECDOTE

Cats are rather delicate creatures and they are subject to a good many different ailments, but I never heard of one who suffered from insomnia.

(Joseph Wood Krutch)

Secret Weapon

During the dark days of the Blitz, the *Daily Telegraph* invited its readers to write in with ideas and inventions to help the war effort. Over 40,000 people responded, including one bright spark who suggested, in all seriousness, that the best way to tackle the waves of enemy bombers that filled the skies over Britain each night was to make sure that every RAF fighter plane carried a cat in the cockpit. His point was that cats can see clearly in the dark, so if the pilot aimed his gun in whichever direction the animal was looking, he was certain to bring down one of the enemy. It didn't seem to have occurred to the inventor of this secret weapon that the cat might be looking at one of our own aircraft at the time.

SNUFFED IT

Charles Dickens' cat Williamina – originally christened William by mistake – used to extinguish the candles in her master's study with her paw if she felt that he was paying too much attention to his work and not enough to her. An explanation perhaps of why Dickens' last book, *The Mystery of Edwin Drood*, was never finished, leaving his readers in the dark.

The cat appears to have feelings only for himself, loves only conditionally and only enters into relations [with people] in order to abuse them.

(COUNT DE BUFFON, *Natural History*, 1767)

_____ PAPAL BULL _____

The Middle Ages was no time to be a cat. Identified with witchcraft and pagan worship, the unfortunate creature found itself blamed for almost any misfortune going, including the Black Death. Millions were slaughtered in a series of grotesque atrocities staged throughout Europe. The Church gave its official blessing to these acts when, in 1484, Pope Innocent VIII issued a statement denouncing sorcery and branding the cat as an agent of the Devil.

———————————— ✳ ————————————

Cat Magic

The American magician Carl Hertz pulled a clever publicity stunt
out of the hat when he toured Australia in 1892.
A few days before his show was due to open in Melbourne,
he put the following advertisement into the local newspaper:

'WANTED – 1,000 cats of all descriptions.
Apply at Stage Door, Opera House, with cats at 9 a.m. tomorrow.
One shilling or a free seat for the evening performance
will be given for each cat.'

The next day more than 2000 moggies – practically
the entire cat population of the city –
were delivered to the stage door, mainly by
enthusiastic children. Each cat was promptly garlanded with a neckband
reading 'See Carl Hertz at the Opera House tonight'
and turned loose on the streets. The idea worked like magic,
the cats conjuring up a full house for the rest of
the six-week season.

CAT COMPOSITION

In one of his popular pre-war articles for the London *Evening Standard*, Dean Inge quoted from a child's essay on cats which contained some charmingly simplistic observations about the animal. Among them:

The cat is a quadruped, the legs as usual being at the four corners . . . Do not tease cats, for, firstly, it is wrong so to do, and, secondly, cats have claws, which are longer than people think . . . Cats have nine lives, but these are seldom required in this country because of Christianity.

An old tom who'd lost eight of his lives
Ate his way through a bucket of chives
When Heaven's bell rang
He went out with a bang
That was heard all the way to St Ives.

Cats are a mysterious kind of folk. There is more passing in their minds than we are aware of.

(Sir Walter Scott)

The smallest feline is a masterpiece. (LEONARDO DA VINCI)

A survey in 1980 revealed that neutered toms live twice as long as un-neutered ones. But they only have half the fun.

Lotta Bottle

Vincenzo D'Aloia, an Italian farmer, was puzzled by the low milk yield from his one and only cow, even more so when the vet confirmed that the animal was in perfect health. There seemed to be only one explanation. So one night Vincenzo lay in wait in his barn to catch whoever it was who was stealing his milk. At first light the door of the barn was pushed open an inch or two and in crept the farmer's cat. Without a moment's hesitation it went over to the cow, jumped on to the milking-stool and helped itself to a breakfast pinta straight from the udder.

Cat mighty dignified till de dog come by. (American Negro proverb)

ʽBATCAT

A correspondent from Sligo in Ireland wrote on 20 September 1872:

I shall send you particulars of an incident which I was an eye-witness of recently, and which struck me very forcibly as an instance or proof of animal sagacity. A bulldog had seized a small terrier by the throat, and could not be made to let go his hold. A large crowd had collected, and, happening to be passing, I also became a spectator. Several people were by this time beating and trying to separate them, when all of a sudden a cat who lived in the house, and who always was fed with the terrier, made a spring through the crowd, and fastening on the bull-dog's head and throat, tore him in such a fearful way that he was compelled to let go the terrier, who was very nearly choked, but by kind treatment he was revived. What made it more remark-able the cat had kittens at the time.

From *Anecdotes in Natural History*, 1873.

Cut!

During the making of the epic movie *Cleopatra* in 1962, a passionate love scene between Richard Burton and Elizabeth Taylor, alias Antony and Cleopatra, was interrupted by strange noises on the soundtrack. On the playback these were identified as cats miaowing, though there was no sign of any animals around. The director ordered a search to be made, in the course of which a large part of the set was dismantled, and underneath one of Cleopatra's thirty-two beds was found a stray cat and her litter of kittens. The cat, which like the amorous Egyptian queen had obviously been sleeping around, not only kept two of Hollywood's highest paid stars off the job, but also cost the film company £3000 to re-build the set.